MRep
PRP

The Fort on Fourth Street

A Story about the Six Simple Machines

by Lois Spangler

illustrated by Christina Wald

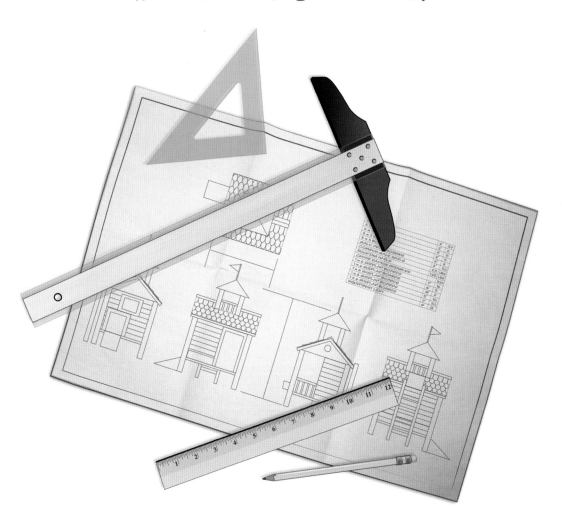

This is the yard on Fourth Street
where I'm building a fort that will be very neat!
Who will help me build it today,
and what will I need to make a fun place to play?

This is the fort that we will build by hand;
with Grandpa's help, we'll build it as planned.
I'll use imagination to create fun spaces.
It will even include some secret places.

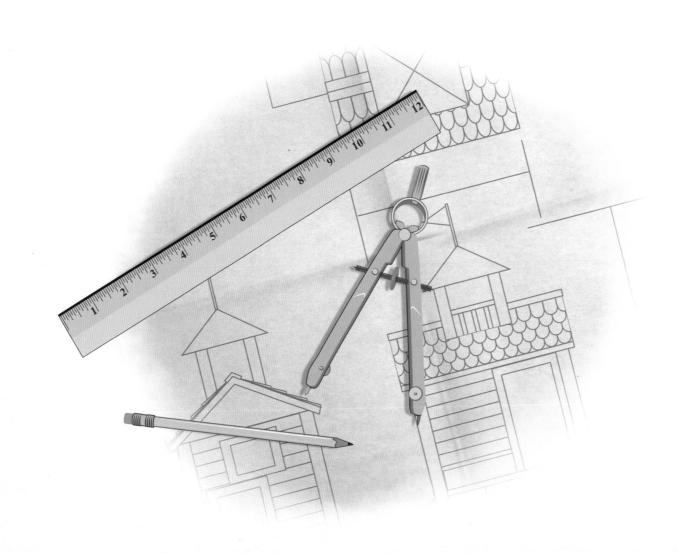

These are the wheels and axles
that move my wagon without hassles.
It carries wood in a great, big mound,
with wheels that make a squeaky sound.

The hands that use simple machines to build the fort on Fourth Street.

This is Grandpa's saw, which is a wedge.
Watch your fingers—it has a sharp edge!
It's bumpy and prickly and cuts the wood,
making each board fit as it should.

SKE-E-E!

And my wagon makes a squeaky sound, when the wheels go round and round, pulled by the hands that use simple machines to build the fort on Fourth Street.

These are the screws that I place in the wood,
tight and solid, so they'll stay in for good.
A rough spiral thread winds around the screw,
joining wood together as the screw pushes through.

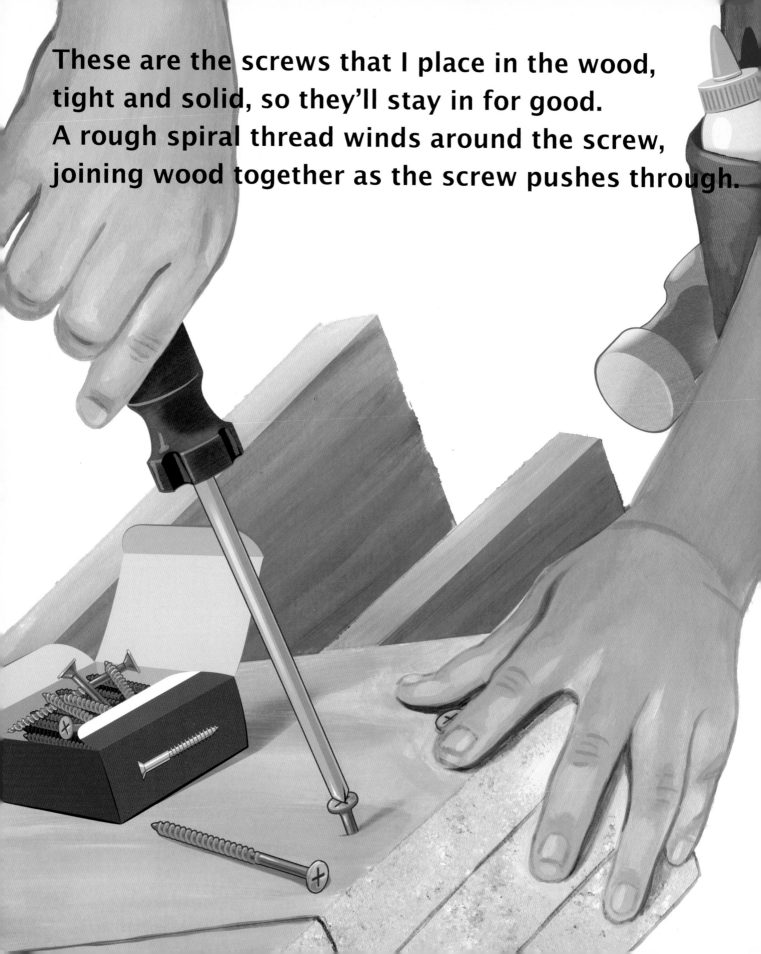

Grandpa's saw cuts the wood,
making each board fit as it should.

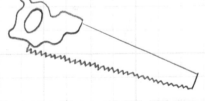

SKE-E-E!

And my wagon makes a squeaky sound,
when the wheels go round and round,

pulled by the hands that use
simple machines to build the
fort on Fourth Street.

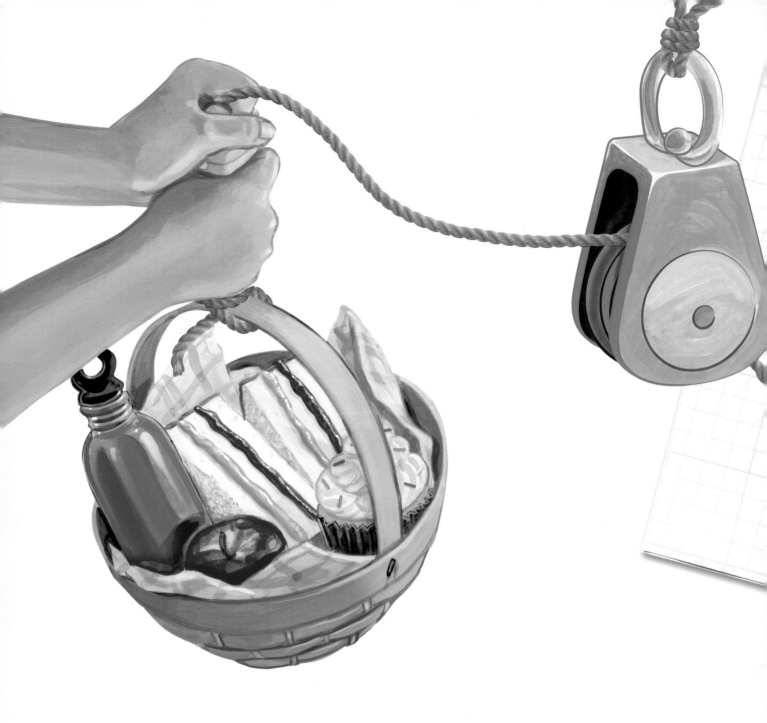

This is the pulley that brings up the treats,
so yummy and sweet that we love to eat.
A basket rises with the force applied
when Grandpa pulls the rope nearby.

You can count the screws deep in the wood,
tight and solid—they'll stay in for good.

Grandpa's saw cuts the wood,
making each board fit as it should.

And my wagon makes a squeaky sound,
when the wheels go round and round,

pulled by the hands that use
simple machines to build the
fort on Fourth Street.

SKE-E-E!

This is the lever that moves a rock
so easily, it is quite a shock!
The rock rolls away and the land is clear,
allowing me to stand quite near.

I use the pulley to bring up the treats,
so yummy and sweet, that we love to eat.

You can count the screws deep in the wood,
tight and solid—they'll stay in for good.

Grandpa's saw cuts the wood,
making each board fit as it should.

SKE-E-E!

And my wagon makes a squeaky sound,
when the wheels go round and round,

pulled by the hands that use simple machines
to build the fort on Fourth Street.

This is the ramp that goes up to the port,
a special opening for those who are short.
Our ramp to the port is an inclined plane,
getting us safely over bumpy terrain.

The lever is used to clear the land,
making a place for me to stand.

I use the pulley to bring up the treats,
so yummy and sweet, that we love to eat.

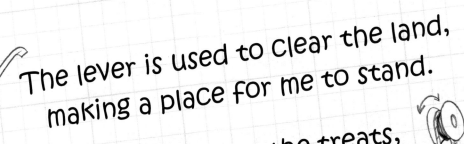

You can count the screws deep in the wood,
tight and solid—they'll stay in for good.

Grandpa's saw cuts the wood,
making each board fit as it should.

SKE-E-E!

And my wagon makes a squeaky sound,
when the wheels go round and round,

pulled by the hands that use simple machines
to build the fort on Fourth Street.

At last, I look around and what do I see?
Six simple machines used to build a fort for me!
We used wheels and axles, a wedge, some screws,
a pulley, a lever, and an inclined plane, too!

We have a ramp that goes up to the port,
a special opening for those who are short.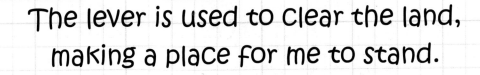

The lever is used to clear the land,
making a place for me to stand.

I use the pulley to bring up the treats,
so yummy and sweet, that we love to eat.

You can count the screws deep in the wood,
tight and solid—they'll stay in for good.

Grandpa's saw cuts the wood,
making each board fit as it should.

SKE-E-E!

And my wagon makes a squeaky sound,
when the wheels go round and round,

pulled by the hands that use simple machines
to build the fort on Fourth Street.

Simple machines, of which we used six,
have few or no moving parts to fix.
They're easy to use and easy to stow,
making it simple when we're on the go!

There are six simple machines that I count.
Can YOU find the correct amount?

We have a ramp that goes up to the port,
a special opening for those who are short.

The lever is used to clear the land,
making a place for me to stand.

I use the pulley to bring up the treats,
so yummy and sweet, that we love to eat.

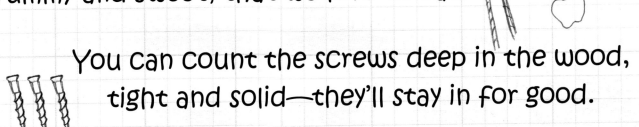

You can count the screws deep in the wood,
tight and solid—they'll stay in for good.

Grandpa's saw cuts the wood,
making each board fit as it should.

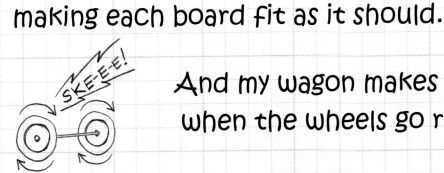

SKE-E-E!

And my wagon makes a squeaky sound,
when the wheels go round and round,

pulled by the hands that use simple machines
to build the fort on Fourth Street.

Simple machines made work easier today,
giving us a place to rest and play.
The fort, for us, is number one,
and will be a place for lots of fun!

Simple machines, of which we use six,
with few or no moving parts to fix.

There are six simple machines that I count.
Can YOU find the correct amount?

We have a ramp that goes up to the port,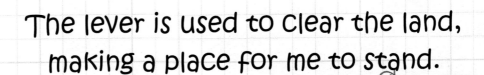
a special opening for those who are short.

The lever is used to clear the land,
making a place for me to stand.

I use the pulley to bring up the treats,
so yummy and sweet, that we love to eat.

You can count the screws deep in the wood,
tight and solid—they'll stay in for good.

Grandpa's saw cuts the wood,
making each board fit as it should.

And my wagon makes a squeaky sound,
when the wheels go round and round,

pulled by the hands that use simple machines
to build the fort on Fourth Street.

This is the fort on Fourth Street,
a special place that's really neat,
built with tools known as simple machines—
a masterpiece, which is now . . .

. . . Kathleen's!

For Creative Minds

Simple Machines

Simple machines have been used for hundreds of years. There are six simple machines—the wedge, wheel and axle, lever, inclined plane, screw, and pulley. They have few or no moving parts and they make work easier. When you use simple machines, you use a force—a push or a pull—to make something move over a distance. There are six types of simple machines. Use the color coding to match the machine's description to its picture.

A **lever** is a stiff bar that turns on a fixed point called a fulcrum. When one side of the lever is pushed down, the other side of the lever lifts up. A lever helps to lift or move things.

An inclined plane is a slanted surface that connects a lower level to a higher level. Objects can be pushed or pulled along the inclined plane to move them from a high place to a low place, or a low place to a high place.

A **pulley** has a grooved wheel and rope to raise and lower a load. Pulling on the rope causes the wheel to turn and raise the object on the other end of the rope.

A screw has an inclined plane (a thread) wrapped around a shaft. The screw's thread interlocks with an object so that the screw cannot be easily pulled out. A screw holds two or more things together.

A **wheel and axle** is a wheel with a rod (the axle) through its center. A wheel and axle help move things by rolling instead of sliding or dragging.

A wedge is an object with at least one slanting side. A wedge is pushed into a single object or between two objects. A wedge can hold things in place or force things apart.

Match the Machines

Which of these are levers, wedges, pulleys, inclined planes, screws, or wheels and axles?

Answers: **levers**: see-saw, hammer claw, nutcracker   **wedges**: knife, axe   **pulleys**: clothes line   **inclined planes**: ramp in sidewalk, ramp on the back of truck   **screws**: bottom of a light bulb, cork screw   **wheel & axles**: windmill, wheel

Measuring Tools

In addition to the simple machines, Kathleen and her grandfather used measuring tools when building the fort. Which tool would you use to measure the following:

1. Kathleen used screws every six inches (15 cm). Which measuring tool do you think she used? Why?

2. Grandpa cut wood into 5-foot sections (1.5 m). Which measuring tool do you think he used? Why?

3. Grandpa measured a 35 degree angle on a board. Which measuring tool would he use? Why?

4. Kathleen measured one of Grandpa's boards. It was exactly 36 inches long. Which measuring tool did she use? Why?

5. Grandpa had some extra wood. Kathleen asked her Grandpa to cut four circles out of the wood. Which tool would Grandpa use to measure the circles? Why?

yard stick

ruler

protractor

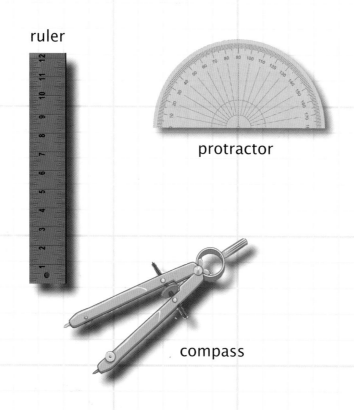

compass

Answers: 1: ruler, 2: measuring tape,
3: protractor, 4: yard stick, 5: compass

measuring tape

Hands On: Building a Fort

Before you get started, think about what kind of fort you want to build.
- Do you want your fort to be inside or outside?
- Are you building a temporary fort or a permanent fort?
- How many people should fit in the fort?
- What materials do you need to build the fort?
- How will you hold the materials together?
- Draw a picture of what your fort will look like.
- Can you scale your picture using measuring tools? For example, in your drawing, one inch could represent one foot. This drawing can be your "guide" when you start to build your fort.

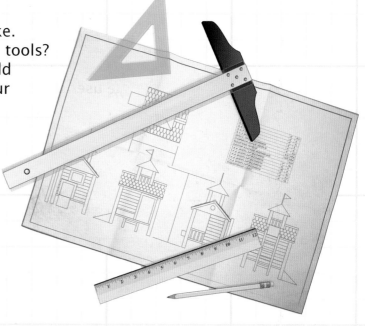

Build your fort!
- Make sure you have permission and always follow safety rules.
- Who will help you build the fort?
- Gather together all the materials you need.
- Do you need any simple machines to make your fort?
- Where can you find simple machines?
- Who will help you use them?
- What are your first steps in building the fort?
- As you are building, do you want to add extra materials?

Look at your finished fort:
- Does your fort look as you thought it would?
- Draw your fort now and compare it to the drawing you made before you built it.
- Did you have to make any changes to your fort's design?
- If so, what did you change while you were building? Why?
- Can you measure your fort?
  - How tall is it?
  - How long are the sides?
  - How many "rooms" does it have?
  - What else can you measure?
- How many people do you think can fit inside your fort?

With love to my husband Larry, son Robert, daughter-in-law Carmen, and my mother Madelon. They are my inspiration and I am eternally grateful for their continued support—LS

Thanks to educators at the Franklin Institute for verifying the accuracy of the information in this book.

Library of Congress Cataloging-in-Publication Data

Spangler, Lois, 1947-
    The fort on Fourth Street : a story about the six simple machines / by Lois Spangler ; illustrated by Christina Wald.
        pages cm
    Summary: Building a fort in the backyard, a grandfather and granddaughter get help from six simple machines: lever, pulley, inclined plane, wheel and axle, screw, and wedge.
    ISBN 978-1-60718-620-5 (english hardcover) -- ISBN 978-1-60718-632-8 (english pbk.) -- ISBN 978-1-60718-644-1 (english ebook (downloadable)) -- ISBN 978-1-60718-668-7 (interactive english/spanish ebook (web-based)) -- ISBN 978-1-60718-717-2 (spanish hardcover) -- ISBN 978-1-60718-656-4 (spanish ebook (downloadable)) [1. Stories in rhyme. 2. Building--Fiction. 3. Simple machines--Fiction. 4. Machinery--Fiction. 5. Grandfathers--Fiction.] I. Wald, Christina, illustrator. II. Spangler, Lois, 1947- Fortaleza de la calle cuatro. III. Title.
    PZ8.3.S734Fo 2013
    [E]--dc23
                              2012045128

Lexile® Level: 920
Curriculum keywords: adapted story with cumulative rhyme, simple machines/tools

Manufactured in China, June, 2013
This product conforms to CPSIA 2008
First Printing

Sylvan Dell Publishing
Mt. Pleasant, SC 29464
www.SylvanDellPublishing.com